Refresh!

A Therapeutic Devotional

ROBYN C. HILL, MA, PCC

Love Clones Publishing
www.lcpublishing.net

Printed in the United States of America

First Printing, 2015

ISBN: 978-0692473856

New Living Translation

Publishers:
Love Clones Publishing
Dallas, TX
www.lcpublishing.net

ACKNOWLEDGMENTS

I want to acknowledge my parents, Larry and Bonita McLemore, who always encouraged my creativity and never discouraged me from dreaming. Because of the values that you have instilled in me, I have never been afraid to be myself and have the audacity to make those dreams a reality. I love you both immeasurably!

INTRODUCTION

Why Refresh?

Thank you for taking time to Refresh! It is my personal and professional mission to give people tools to improve their quality of life. Many people are living their lives without experiencing the satisfaction of living a fulfilling lifestyle. It is a necessity to engage in activities that increase the appreciation for living from day to day. I named this book, Refresh, to facilitate a daily activity that will give the day more value and worth. According to the Merriam-Webster Online dictionary, the word "refresh" means "to restore strength." It also defines it as a way "to update or renew." As we go through daily stressors and negative life experiences, it is important that we learn ways to refresh.

Daily stressors and negative life experiences impact how we feel and how we function in the major areas of our lives – home, work, and relationships. It is important to determine what your daily stressors are because you have to know what is draining you.

When we are unaware of these stressors, we blindly go on through our daily routines, unaware that we are approaching empty. By the time we realize all that is stressing to us, we find ourselves crashing into a proverbial wall that will deplete our emotions, reduce our functioning, and require a longer recovery period for healing to occur.

Negative life experiences are a little more severe than your daily life stressors. These are events that leave a bad memory etched into your mind, and even your spirit. These experiences may include losses: whether they are relationships, finances, possessions, or status, difficult transitions, or a traumatic memory. We often go through life trying to force a sense of "letting go," but if we are candid, we know that we can never get the memory etched out of our minds. So when we are reminded of the pain, it pulls on our negative emotions. The more severe the experience, the more severe the impact our emotions will have on our ability to function in the 3 key areas of home, work, and relationships.

This is why it is imperative that we learn to Refresh. As a part of our daily routine, we must learn how to incorporate activities that help us to restore our strength. Daily stressors and negative life experiences weaken us slowly as we go about our day. As you continually pour yourself out at work and with your families, incorporating activities that refresh you will help you maintain the physical, emotional, and spiritual strength. In my first book, A Healing Conversation: Beginning Steps Towards Dealing With A Painful Past, I explore several different methods to help with expressing and coping with emotions in a healthy manner. In this book, I want to dig deeper into the concept of meditation by using a process I call "therapeutic devotion."

Why Therapeutic?

Well, I am a therapist. I work with clients who have reached their emotional breaking point because they have allowed the daily stressors and negative life experiences to go on unaddressed. There is a need to add to our skill set activities that help us cope with negative emotions.

There are a plethora of tools that clinicians use in therapy to help deal cope with emotions. The therapist's goal is to teach skills that will help you tell your story, identify your emotions, and gain a better understanding of yourself in order to help you to feel better and cope effectively. Ultimately, we want to help you reduce the frequency and severity of negative emotions, while increasing the frequency and longevity of positive ones. All the tools we use are to achieve these goals. The tool that I am incorporating into this book is the process of journaling.

I love to encourage journaling as a therapeutic exercise for several reasons. First and foremost, it gets you to express your innermost thoughts. For some reason, we become so much more expressive when the pen hits the paper. I have had clients that were not talkative at all and it was very difficult to get an understanding of how they were feeling about the issue which led to their presence in counseling. Even as I suggest a journaling activity in session, they look skeptical stating that they don't know what to write. But, I will hand them the paper and pen, tell them to write, stop the conversation, turn my back – and the pen gets going. Before you know it, the client has written a two-page letter expressing thoughts and emotions that they struggled to utter aloud.

The key to learning any new skill is repetition. To truly master this skill, you will need to do it daily, in spite of how you feel about the skill. Actually, the best time to learn any skill is when you are not at your worst because it is difficult to integrate a new skill when you are emotionally drained. When you start incorporating a new skill during the less stressful times, it increases the likelihood that you will successfully use it when times get more unbearable.

There are varying opinions on the length of time a new habit should be practiced for it to become automatic. Popular belief is that it takes about 21 days, while other psychological studies have found that a minimum of two months is the most effective time span. For this book, I decided to take a spiritual approach and go with a total of 40 days. The number 40 has been a significant number during Biblical times, so it just seems right for this particular activity, which is a therapeutic devotional journal.

Why Devotion?

We are all created holistically as physical, mental, and spiritual beings. In order for there to be balance in our lives, we must assess and care for ourselves mentally, physically, and spiritually. Historically, however, there has been a schism between mental and spiritual care. Psychological theory came onto the scene as an alternative to address the issues of the psyche, which means the soul, that were not being addressed by organized religion. But as the world of psychology has developed, leading scholars are finding that counseling is more effective when spirituality is incorporated. To ignore spirituality is to ignore a part of your being and regardless of your spiritual orientation, there is a soul that needs to be nurtured. Hence, it is necessary to learn how to engage in spiritual practices.

I like to describe our being as a baby mobile with three parts hanging from it – those parts are the mind, the body, and the spirit. When you pull one of the parts out of position, the other two are out of position as well. We, as a society, have become very well versed in things we need in order to become more physically fit and healthy. Additionally, there are more and more teachings on mental wellness to reduce the negative impacts of mental illness. Major corporations are creating all kinds of employee programs promoting physical health and offering free mental health counseling as a part of the benefits packages. But when it comes to spiritual care, we are kind of left to our own devices, as if it is a social gaffe to mention it outside of our places of worship.

One of the most essential practices or disciplines that encompasses spirituality is the act of prayer. The focus of this devotional is to help you become more relational in your prayers with God. A lot of people are very skilled in listing grievances to God, while others are too intimidated to engage with Him at all. But the true act of prayer is meant to be more engaging and interactive; it is a discipline that allows you to move past just mere thoughts and participate in spiritual communication with the Creator. My goal for you is that you not only learn how to talk to God, but also how to listen for a response through meditation.

Therapeutic Devotion

Therapeutic Devotion is a term that I use to describe the utilization of scriptural reflection as a mindfulness tool. Mindfulness is a meditative skill common in Buddhism and frequently utilized in therapy to foster relaxation and focus. The task is to reflect on a written passage or an object, giving it all of your attention and shutting out all external distraction. Mindfulness is useful in reducing anxiety and elevating moods. Therapeutic Devotions focus on the reflection of a scripture to bring about a therapeutic understanding and to improve positive mood. This task is broken down in three steps.

The first step of this skill set is to read a scripture and the following passage. I primarily utilize the New Living Translation because I like how it reads and flows. Just focus on what you are reading and process what is being said in the passage. Your goal is to close your mind to all external distractions and meditate on what you have read. This skill takes practice, and with time you should be able to increase your ability to focus on the moment. Take the next few minutes, go to a quiet place, and read the following devotion. Then take 2-3 minutes to reflect on what you read.

The second step is to engage in prayer through the journaling process. Each devotion will focus on applying scripture to an area of mental health and symptoms. After you take a few minutes to reflect on the passage, then take time to write a prayer to God on your reflection. Write out your prayer on the page that opens with "Dear God" and write as much as is on your heart. Share how the devotion applies to you and discuss this with God.

The third and final step is to tune your ear for a response from God. After you have written your prayer reflecting on the devotion, take a few more minutes to sit in silence. Clear your mind and shut out distractions, while listening for God to respond to your prayer. Then, pick up your pen and start writing what you sense God is saying to you on the page that starts with "My child." Do not fixate on whether this is God or yourself talking, just write. As with the other parts of this skill, this too will improve with practice and time. The key is to position yourself spiritually and still yourself to communicate with God. Ultimately the goal is to help you regulate your emotions by engaging in a spiritual activity. Do not put pressure on yourself to be perfect – as I have said before, this takes practice. Hopefully, after you have completed this journal, you will be able to continue this discipline on your own. Let's go and enjoy your moments with God!

DAY 1

Romans 12:2 "Don't copy the behavior and customs of this world, but let God transform you into a new person by changing the way you think. Then you will know what God wants you to do, and you will know how good and pleasing and perfect his will really is."

God's method of transforming you is by changing the way you think. This is because our thoughts shape our behaviors. Our thoughts are formulated by our attitudes and beliefs. These attitudes and beliefs stem from our life experiences. God wants to address those life experiences that have caused us to view the world the way we do. These experiences are often those dark and ungodly memories that have caused us to believe that nothing good can come out of life. God wants to get into those dark places of our mind with us, to work through those memories, and give us a new interpretation of life.

Dear God,

My Child,

Day 2

James 2:2-5 "We all make many mistakes, but those who control their tongues can also control themselves in every other way. We can make a large horse turn around and go wherever we want by means of a small bit in its mouth. And a tiny rudder makes a huge ship turn wherever the pilot wants it to go, even though the winds are strong. So also, the tongue is a small thing, but what enormous damage it can do. A tiny spark can set a great forest on fire."

The way we talk to ourselves has a great effect on how we live our lives. Negative self-talk can turn our lives in a negative direction. We no longer expect good things to happen for us. We tend to draw towards the negative, unproductive things in life. But we can also turn our lives in a different direction by changing our thoughts to positive self-talk. Through affirmations, we begin to view the world in a more positive light and begin to expect new opportunities. "A tiny spark can set a great forest on fire" hence what you say to and about yourself will consume your life. Be consumed with positivity!

Dear God,

My Child,

DAY 3

Psalm 131:1-2 "LORD, my heart is not proud; my eyes are not haughty. I don't concern myself with matters too great or awesome for me. But I have stilled and quieted myself, just as a small child is quiet with its mother. Yes, like a small child is my soul within me."

Anxiety often consumes the mind with things that are too great for you to deal with at the moment. What matters are beyond your control which are causing you to search for solutions? Stop allowing these thoughts to race through your mind. Instead of focusing on these things, reflect on how God has been sustaining you. Look at what needs are being met and allow those reflections to satisfy your soul. Reflect daily in order to nurture contentment.

Dear God,

My Child,

Day 4

I Thessalonians 4:11-12 "Make it your goal to live a quiet life, minding your own business and working with your hands...Then people who are not Christians will respect the way you live, and you will not need to depend on others."

External stressors are major contributors to anxiety and depression. Oftentimes, the external stressors are unnecessary people or things we allow to infiltrate our lives. We allow these things in our lives because we are trying to add superficial value to our existence. However, if you remove the stressors and focus on living a quiet life, you will see a reduction in the negative emotions that you are experiencing. Additionally, you will no longer be dependent upon outside people and things to add value to you. Assess your life right now – what unnecessary stressors can be removed? Is it people... is it material possessions... is it lofty expectations?

Dear God,

My Child,

DAY 5

I Kings 19:11-12 "'Go out and stand before me on the mountain,' the LORD told him. And as Elijah stood there, the LORD passed by, and a mighty windstorm hit the mountain. It was such a terrible blast that the rocks were torn loose, but the LORD was not in the wind. After the wind there was an earthquake, but the LORD was not in the earthquake. And after the earthquake there was a fire, but the LORD was not in the fire. And after the fire there was the sound of a gentle whisper..."

We are in the age of the "Pep Rallies." The "you don't want to miss this," "come get empowered, inspired," "get a fresh word," and "you will never be the same" productions, as if there were big flashing signs saying "Encouragement here!!!" We go from one high energy, music filled, and catch-phrase event to another looking to get something to help us make it through our days, our lives. There is nothing wrong with encouragement but sometimes it offers little more than emotional stimulation to hold you over until the next emotional stimulation, which is actually distracting you from what you really need - an intimate one-on-one encounter with the Almighty creator, God Himself.

When you are still in that quiet place, then He may whisper something to you that is just for you. And God's presence will transform any situation and any mindset. The Bible says "My sheep know my voice," so what is He saying to YOU? Have you stilled yourself today?

Dear God,

My Child,

DAY 6

Romans 8:26-27 "In the same way, the Spirit helps us in our weakness. We do not know what we ought to pray for, but the Spirit himself intercedes for us through wordless groans. And he who searches our hearts knows the mind of the Spirit, because the Spirit intercedes for God's people in accordance with the will of God."

The Spirit of God helps us communicate our weaknesses in prayer by interceding for us. However, we often don't recognize when something is wrong, putting on a happy face, pushing through, pretending that we are content. When we avoid our emotions by denying our problems, we avoid communicating to the Spirit of God what is wrong. Then we don't give the Spirit of God the permission to fully do His work in bringing about our healing. It's okay to feel. It's okay to cry. You don't always need words because your tears will communicate with God.

What are you avoiding? Let the emotions out, so that the Spirit of God can search your heart and intercede on your behalf.

Dear God,

My Child,

DAY 7

Psalm 40:3a "He has given me a new song to sing. A Hymn of praise to our God."

We often retell our hurts over and over as if we are rehearsing a sad song. The problem is, the more we repeat the pain and the more we repeat the negative thinking patterns that developed as a result of the pain. We relate to the pain and become comfortable in it, so much so we become dependent on the familiarity of the pain. It is time to sever the relationship and stop singing the same sad song.
What has been your song of despair? What does your new song of praise look like? Ask God to give you a new song.

Dear God,

My Child,

Day 8

Ecclesiastes 7:20 "Not a single person on earth is always good and never sins."

Solomon has been recognized as the wisest man to walk the earth, and this was one of the conclusions he drew from his life experience. That is because it is a negative assumption called generalization that uses the words always and never. When we generalize, we create negative emotions because of the expectation that something will or should always/never happen. It is an unrealistic expectation to believe that anyone is always good or will never sin.

Release yourself from the expectation of perfection. Allow yourself and the people around you to have faults. When we accept the notion that no one is perfect, we reduce the intensity of negative emotions when failures happen. Take the pressure off.

Dear God,

My Child,

DAY 9

Ecclesiastes 5:3 "Too much activity gives you restless dreams; too many words make you a fool."

In this day and age, we can get overwhelmed with daily responsibilities. If we aren't completing long to-do lists for the day, we are up all night thinking about the things for tomorrow's list. "What am I going to wear?" "Oh, I can't forget to buy..." "I have to return that phone call." Before you know it, you're struggling with initiating or maintaining sleep because your mind is preoccupied with racing thoughts.

Without a good night's sleep, we become susceptible to negative emotions. Lack of sleep has been associated with irritability, anxiety, and depression. Additionally, you may experience physical health problems because your body is not allowed to fully rejuvenate. It is important to make rest a priority. Is busy-ness interfering with your sleep? What can you change about your daily schedule to help put your mind at ease at night?

Dear God,

My Child,

Day 10

Deuteronomy 31:8 "Do not be afraid or discouraged, for the Lord will personally go ahead of you. He will be with you; he will neither fail you nor abandon you."

Dealing with difficult situations can be very intimidating. Many times, we avoid confrontation because we don't know where it will lead. Whether we are dealing with a relationship, a current situation, or trying to deal with the past; in order to resolve it we have to go through feelings of anxiety and uncertainty. The situation can be minor or a very difficult issue that is being addressed; but the impulse is to avoid it, so that we don't have to feel bad. However, there is comfort in knowing that the God of the Universe is going before you as you approach that issue. He is with you to ease your fears and comfort you.

Dear God,

My Child,

DAY 11

Proverbs 3:24 "You can go to bed without fear; you will lie down and sleep soundly."

Daily worries can be excessive and are a sign of anxiety. Fear is the root of anxiety. Fear can originate from a bad experience but it also stems from an irrational thought that results in exaggerated expectations. Our imagination can make a worry become a tragedy, as we play out the worst case scenarios in our minds. This is called "catastrophizing," where we overstress a negative situation. What do you worry about? What about that do you fear? What if the fear comes true, how does that change your life? Now hand those worries to God and go to bed without fear.

Dear God,

My Child,

Day 12

Isaiah 30:18 "So the Lord must wait for you to come to him so he can show you his love and compassion. For the Lord is a faithful God. Blessed are those who wait for his help."

Entering into relationship and communication with God can be intimidating. Oftentimes, we fear His presence because we don't know what He will expect of us. We also may have a grievance with God, feeling as though He has let us down at some point in our lives. We may have done or been through some things that may discourage us in communicating with Him. But lack of connection with God causes us to shut down our spiritual senses. A part of our being (mind/body/spirit) is not allowed expression, which often times results in negative emotions and physical ailments. We don't realize the impact that avoiding God has on our entire being.

The scripture says He is waiting for us to come to Him. Not because He wants to reject us, but because He wants to reveal His love and compassion to us...to you. And He is faithful, meaning He is never changing – this is who He is, God waiting to pour out love and compassion. Go to Him and open yourself up to receive what He has for you.

Dear God,

My Child,

Day 13

1 Samuel 16:7 "But the LORD said to Samuel, 'Don't judge by his appearance or height, for I have rejected him. The LORD doesn't make decisions the way you do! People judge by outward appearance, but the LORD looks at a person's thoughts and intentions.'"

We often limit ourselves by the expectations that society have placed on us. There are societal norms that suggest what should be considered attractive, successful, or even desirable. Even amongst our spiritual affiliations, we can find ourselves not measuring up because we have become subject to unreasonable expectations. What makes the expectations unreasonable is that they are unattainable or merely because they are useless. Who told you to live up to superficial standards? Why do you measure your worth by them?

God says He doesn't qualify us based on our limited human understanding of quality. He sets a standard of worth based on the person He created you to be. He looks at your core self, your innermost thoughts and desires. Are you judging yourself by society's standards, or by God's?

Dear God,

My Child,

Day 14

Jeremiah 31:37 "Just as the heavens cannot be measured and the foundation of the earth cannot be explored, so I will not consider casting them away forever for their sins. I, the LORD, have spoken!"

Shame can make us feel as if we are cast-aways, unable to go to God because we can't face Him. But God says, just as you cannot measure the heavens, He cannot even fathom casting you away for something you have done. Bring your shame to Him and let Him embrace you and cast away your shame.

Dear God,

My Child,

DAY 15

Psalm 32:8, 9 "The LORD says, "I will guide you along the best pathway for your life. I will advise you and watch over you. Do not be like a senseless horse or mule that needs a bit and bridle to keep it under control."

When it comes to making important life choices, we tend to look to so many outside sources for recommendations and guidance. There is nothing wrong with seeking wise counsel, but it is equally important to make decisions for yourself. Outside people will give you daily instructions for your life from their vantage point. They do not see the future God has set up for you.

It is more important that you consult God on your day-to-day and life decisions. God likens the need for outside confirmation on your own decisions as that to a horse who has to be guided by a bit in its mouth. A horse in this situation is not free, because it is subject to whoever is holding the bit. Just the same, you are not free if you can only move when given instruction and guidance from others. Being in tune with God allows you to be free and live God's plan to the fullest. Besides, He says He has the "best" path for you.

Who is holding the "bit" in your life?

Dear God,

My Child,

DAY 16

Isaiah 46:4 "I will be your God throughout your lifetime -- until your hair is white with age. I made you, and I will care for you. I will carry you along and save you."

One of the hardest hurdles for establishing trust in any relationship is trusting that the person will not leave. Fear of abandonment can plague many relationships. This is because it often has roots in the perception of a very important relationship not being available in a very important time of need.

Even more difficult is the perception that God was not present in a difficult situation. Have you ever felt that God was not near when you needed Him? It is time to talk with Him about it.

Dear God,

My Child,

DAY 17

Philippians 4:8 "Finally, brothers, whatever is true, whatever is noble, whatever is right, whatever is pure, whatever is lovely, whatever is admirable--if anything is excellent or praiseworthy--think about such things."

One trait of depression and anxiety is the subconscious ignorance of positive emotions. The conditions cause us to focus on the experience of negative moods. It becomes very easy to express feeling down and all the symptoms associated with it. As these conditions persist, it becomes harder to recall good times.

We have to become conscious of the things that make us feel good. In those times, however brief, that we feel good we need to truly experience them. Be in the moment. Experience smiling, purity, laughing, calmness.... Whatever is lovely, take a pause, think about it, and experience it in that moment.

Dear God,

My Child,

DAY 18

Hosea 6:6b "...I want you to know Me more than I want burnt offerings."

When we think of spirituality, we tend to assume that it always requires religious rituals. However, rituals don't always engage our spiritual nature. In fact, they can be distractions to getting in tune with our spiritual senses. It is good to incorporate rituals as a means of engaging your spiritual community, but it is not meant to replace your personal spiritual enlightenment. Getting to know God is a personal endeavor and is more important than rituals. Remember, spirituality is a part of our being and we must tend to it effectively.

Dear God,

My Child,

Day 19

Isaiah 40:30, 31 "Even youths will become exhausted, and young men will give up. But those who wait on the LORD will find new strength. They will fly high on wings like eagles. They will run and not grow weary. They will walk and not faint."

Have you ever felt overwhelmed? Have you felt like giving up? The stressors of life can wear you down and exhaust your ability to bounce back. It is not uncommon and many people have felt like quitting or didn't know how to go on. It is important to draw your resiliency from where you draw your hope. Allow God to restore your strength and zeal for life.

Ask Him to refresh you and to refresh you daily.

Dear God,

My Child,

DAY 20

James 4:8 "Draw close to God, and God will draw close to you..."

Do you believe God wants to get to know you? Do you understand God wants to know your deepest secrets? He desires to look at you and all the things you think are ugly about you. It is in those private places that God wants to comfort and guide you. Even when we think we are seeking God, we tend to hide certain parts of ourselves. So what is keeping your guard up? What discourages you from taking steps towards Him? If you take a step, so will He.

Dear God,

My child,

Day 21

Psalm 9:1 "I will praise you, LORD, with all my heart; I will tell of all the marvelous things you have done."

Practicing gratefulness can be a difficult task, especially when you are going through difficulties in life. But it is important to put life problems into perspective. When we list all the good things that we have in life, it helps to deter us from catastrophizing the negative things. Catastrophizing is a thinking error that causes us to magnify a negative life event into something bigger than it is. Reminding yourself of all of the wonderful things God has done for you can help reduce the problem in your perception and help you to improve your mood. Everyday is a good day to count your blessings...

Dear God,

My Child,

DAY 22

Ecclesiastes 5:19 "And it is a good thing to receive wealth from God and the good health to enjoy it. To enjoy your work and accept your lot in life -- this is indeed a gift from God."

Dissatisfaction with work can have a heavy impact on your mental wellness. Do you find yourself not enjoying your work, or maybe just some aspects of it? What would it take to make you enjoy your job more? Maybe you have been out of work. Maybe you are not passionate about what you are doing and need to move into a new professional area. Or you have found yourself a caretaker and are not in a place to work. Whatever your "lot," the key question is: are you satisfied?

To enjoy your work is a gift from God. So we need to discover the root of our dissatisfaction, if there be any. You may need to change your perspective or change your position to truly receive this gift from God.

Dear God,

My Child,

Day 23

2 Peter 1:2 "May God bless you with his special favor and wonderful peace as you come to know Jesus, our God and Lord, better and better."

Have you experienced His wonderful peace? What does it feel like? The scripture says that as you grow in your relationship with God, you will receive this wonderful peace. It requires commitment to knowing God better. It is a relationship that needs to be nurtured like any other. This is a deeper relationship than that of an acquaintance. A better relationship will develop as you spend more time practicing spiritual disciplines like prayer, meditation, worship, and self-reflection. Have you been getting to know Him better?

Dear God,

My Child,

DAY 24

Psalm 147:3 "He heals the brokenhearted, binding up their wounds."

A broken heart can be the most excruciating emotional pain any person can experience. A lost love, grief, broken friendships, or unmet expectations can all result in a broken heart. The pain is felt emotionally with racing and intrusive thoughts, flooded with emotions, and is also felt physically, with aching chest and stomach pains. Sleep can be disturbed and you can find yourself so distracted. God says He heals the brokenhearted. He understands your pain. Show Him your wound. He knows how to help you and heal you.

Dear God,

My Child,

DAY 25

Isaiah 26:3 "You will keep in perfect peace all who trust in you, all whose thoughts are fixed on you!"

Peace is the contrary to anxiety. Anxious thoughts often plague the mind, causing us to worry about things that have not happened yet. These worries can be probable but they are often an exaggeration of negative expectations. Chances are the outcome will not be as bad as predicted. So the best way to manage anxious thoughts is to stop them and replace them with other thoughts. It is good to replace negative thoughts with positive ones. Think about the attributes of God and your developing relationship with Him. Allow the thoughts to create a calm that will fill you.

Dear God,

My Child,

DAY 26

Hebrews 4:16 "So let us come boldly to the throne of our gracious God. There we will receive his mercy, and we will find grace to help us when we need it most."

Come boldly! Sometimes our misperceptions of God keep us from coming to Him with boldness. These misperceptions may have come from a skewed teaching about Him or maybe our own misinterpretation of His character. This causes us to keep emotional and spiritual walls up when going to God about our life. He's not too busy for you. Your problems are not too small. You and your needs are important to Him. So clear the air about your misperceptions, so you can find your boldness.

Dear God,

My Child,

Day 27

Psalm 4:4 "Don't sin by letting anger gain control over you. Think about it overnight and remain silent."

Anger is a natural emotion just like all the others and should not be avoided. The issue is not that something made you angry but the manner in which you may want to express your anger. Anger often escalates when you feel as though you are not being heard. The more you try to get your point across and the more you feel ignored or invalidated, the more intense the anger becomes. Before you know it, you have said or done something out of anger that was hurtful and not representative of your true character. Additionally, what initially made you angry never gets addressed.

The scripture says when you let anger control you, it causes you to act in a way that not good for your soul. Heed the advice to think about what is angering you and remain silent. As you're calming in silence, seek a better way to express the things that anger you.

Dear God,

My Child,

DAY 28

Proverbs 27:19 "As a face is reflected in water, so the heart reflects the person."

Oftentimes, we feel as though our smile hides our pains from the world. But the heart reflects to others the challenges we may be facing. This is why you can look at someone and ask "what's wrong?" – Because you can see that something is going on within that person. We can no longer mask what is on our hearts. If we want the world to see happy and peaceful, then we need to cleanse our hearts from the things that are weighing on us. Are you aware of all that is on your heart? The people you encounter do, even if you don't. Let God reveal your heart to you so you can hand those issues over and gain a new reflection.

Dear God,

My Child,

Day 29

1 Chronicles 28:20 "Then David continued, 'Be strong and courageous, and do the work. Don't be afraid or discouraged, for the LORD God, my God, is with you. He will not fail you or forsake you. He will see to it that all the work related to the Temple of the LORD is finished correctly.' "

Getting emotionally and spiritually healthy can seem like an overwhelming task because it takes work. It requires you to learn new behaviors and to leave your comfort zones. But you can't allow yourself to run from change. Consider how painful it is to stay in the same emotional place. This pain far outweighs the pain of changing and getting healthy. So be strong and courageous, you can do the work! God is with you and will help you.

Dear God,

My Child,

DAY 30

Isaiah 43:19a "For I am about to do a brand-new thing. See, I have already begun! Do you not see it?..."

In life, we get used to accepting the hardships that come to us. We can become so accustomed to being treated poorly or never making progress. Feeling better seems to be a high hope and so we settle for being in the same place, never looking for anything to change.

In order for you to accept and allow change, you have to envision it first. Better will not just fall into your lap, you have to decide what better looks like. What is God trying to show you that He has for you? What keeps you from seeing it?

Dear God,

My Child,

DAY 31

Psalm 149:4-5 "For the LORD delights in his people; he crowns the humble with salvation. Let the faithful rejoice in this honor. Let them sing for joy as they lie on their beds."

Did you know that God delights in you? To delight in something, you have to enjoy it. God enjoys you and everything He created about you. That's a thought to comfort you at night. Repeat that affirmation as you pray and as you sleep. The God of the universe, the God of all creation, delights in you. Your "being" pleases Him. You're worth it to Him. You're His. Take joy in knowing this fact.

Dear God,

My Child,

DAY 32

Galatians 6:9 "So don't get tired of doing what is good. Don't get discouraged and give up, for we will reap a harvest of blessing at the appropriate time."

Over a lifetime, we can learn so many unhealthy ways to get our needs met. When those ways no longer work for us or causes more problems, then we are motivated for change. It is a wonderful thing to choose to be a better person. Don't allow frustrations to cause you to fall back into old behaviors. If they were effective, you would not have chosen to change. Continue to do what is good, and ultimately for your good. More good will return to you, so stay the course.

Dear God,

My Child,

Day 33

Ecclesiastes 10:10 "Since a dull ax requires great strength, sharpen the blade. That's the value of wisdom; it helps you succeed."

When you are not operating at your best, it takes more work to accomplish a task. This is called burn-out and you need to be refreshed. Do what it takes to make you "sharper." Learn how to take a break, engage in relaxation, explore new skills/activities, or schedule a fun night. Doing so will help you to be more successful at the changes you are trying to make in your life.

Dear God,

My Child,

DAY 34

Mark 9:24 "The father instantly replied, "I do believe, but help me not to doubt!"

This was a prayer of a man who was requesting healing from Jesus. This man was in the presence of Jesus, and admitted that he struggled with doubt. Doubting is natural, hiding it is not. We struggle with doubts regularly, but we don't like to recognize them. There is a fear that if we voice doubts, somehow we are speaking negativity into our lives. But when we tell God our doubts, He can meet us there and walk us through it. Share your doubts with God, so that He can help your faith to grow.

Dear God,

My Child,

DAY 35

Jude 1:20 "But you, dear friends, must continue to build your lives on the foundation of your holy faith. And continue to pray as you are directed by the Holy Spirit."

Your foundation for life should be built upon your values and priorities. In error, we tend to make our wants and desires to be our primary focus in life because we are living with our aim at getting our most basic needs met. Our wants and desires do not necessarily match our values. When we focus solely on our wants and desires, we place our priorities on the back burner. We may find ourselves neglecting our true selves and our values for meeting needs in the moment. But we need to place emphasis on what we value.

What do you most value in life? Have your values gotten lost along the way? Glean new values from your faith – your belief system. These values will assist you in your daily decisions and the choices you make. And continue to pray, as the scripture instructs, to help you reinforce your values daily.

Dear God,

My Child,

DAY 36

Psalm 6:3 "I am sick at heart. How long, O LORD, until you restore me?"

Change doesn't always happen in the timespan that we want it to. It can be very frustrating seeing that as time passes, the hurts/behaviors/problems are still there. You may be doing the work, but are still waiting to see the positive results.

The frustration is valid and needs proper expression. If we don't speak about the frustrations in a healthy way and try to ignore it, we will express it negatively. This is how we fall back into old behaviors and ways of thinking. So don't suppress the frustrations. Just as the Psalmist did, voice it.... and then listen for solutions...

Dear God,

My Child,

DAY 37

Ecclesiastes 6:9 "Enjoy what you have rather than desiring what you don't have. Just dreaming about nice things is meaningless; it is like chasing the wind."

Learning to become content with what you have can be very difficult. It is acceptable to want better for yourself. At the same time, don't miss out on the wonderful things that are in your life now. We can overlook the good in our current life when we are consumed with daydreaming for better. The scripture likens daydreaming to chasing the wind, an activity that produces nothing because the wind can't be caught.

Observe your surroundings. What wonderful things you have! It's amazing to see how you've found purpose for all that you have now. Look past the imperfections and find enjoyment in the moment.

Dear God,

My Child,

DAY 38

1 Timothy 1:19 "Cling tightly to your faith in Christ, and always keep your conscience clear. For some people have deliberately violated their consciences; as a result, their faith has been shipwrecked."

There are times that out of frustration, we react to situations in ways that go against our better judgment. This leads to feelings of resentment and guilt. We either feel really bad about ourselves or we refuse to take responsibility and blame others. This can hinder your spiritual walk if you are withholding these negative emotions. Don't allow negative situations to cause you to go against your own values. Be true to yourself, even when it is difficult. It is always good to keep a clear conscious.

Dear God,

My Child,

DAY 39

Psalm 127:2 "It is useless for you to work so hard from early morning until late at night, anxiously working for food to eat; for God gives rest to his loved ones."

Rest and relaxation are so important to maintaining good health – physically, mentally, and spiritually. We often praise people who work hard and can handle multiple tasks but sometimes it is a sign of something less positive. It does not help you to work extra hard and lack rest if it is increasing your anxiety and other negative emotions. This will lead to burnout, which will cause more problems than not getting all your tasks done. Have you learned how to make time to rest? Rest is a gift from God.

Dear God,

My Child,

Day 40

Philippians 1:6 "And I am sure that God, who began the good work within you, will continue his work until it is finally finished on that day when Christ Jesus comes back again."

Take comfort in knowing that what God has chosen to work with you on, He will finish. The scripture says "until it is finally finished." This phrase suggests that the work is a process, meaning it will take time. Do not get discouraged because you are not where you wanted to be at this time. Allow the process to work. In the meantime, reflect on your journey and note all the subtle changes that have occurred along the way. You don't do everything like you used to. Continue to allow God to work on you. It is a continual process, and you are getting better day by day...

Dear God,

My Child,

CONCLUSION

Now How Refreshing Was That?

Thank you so much for choosing to go on this 40 day journey with me. Even though the tasks were simple, I know that the process was not easy. Some things may have resonated with you, while others may not have been as personal. At other times, the topics may have been very difficult to face. And a lot of the times, you may have found yourself getting easily distracted and frustrated. But it is so needed to take all these issues that plague our minds and spirits to God. Trust me, it gets simpler as time goes on and your ability to focus in the moment will continue to improve. Engaging a conversation with God is so vital for our holistic beings – mind, body, and spirit. When we omit the spiritual nature, we dull our senses for everyday tasks. Prayer and meditation help us to set the tone for the day, regulate emotions, and improve our daily choices. Hopefully, you began to experience these subtle changes throughout this 40 day journey.

Now What?

You need to continue with this discipline. Begin with reading a chapter of the Bible a day and reflect on what you read just as you did with this devotional. Then allow God to speak application for your life from the passage. Don't focus on study, this is not Bible study time. This time in reading is specifically for your prayer and meditation. You want to continue engaging in a conversation with God and then positioning yourself to hear from Him. This time is so necessary for your spiritual growth. You need the daily silence and the one-on-one time with Him. As you continue with this discipline, you will become more comfortable and you will find your time with God more fulfilling. You will grow closer and closer to Him and find that your spiritual practices help you regulate emotionally. I hope that you have enjoyed this time and will continue this as a part of your everyday lifestyle.

Now go on and continue in your journey....

ABOUT THE AUTHOR

Robyn Hill is an independently licensed professional clinical counselor (PCC), issued by the State of Ohio Counselor, Social Worker, and Marriage and Family Therapist Board. She studied at Ashland Theological Seminary, where Robyn obtained a Master of Arts Degree in Clinical Pastoral Counseling in 2005.

Robyn Hill has worked in various areas of counseling, including chemical dependency, child and adolescent, residential with severe behaviorally handicapped, and with adults with various mental disorders. She also has experience working with various demographics and understands the needs of these different populations. In 2011, she began Robyn C. Hill Counseling and Professional Development Services, a private practice where she provides culturally and spiritually sensitive counseling in the areas of depression, anxiety, and trauma recovery. In addition to counseling, Robyn Hill offers training and workshops to area organizations on topics of mental wellness. Additionally, she provides clinical services to smaller non-profits agencies to assist them with curriculum and programming development.

In 2012, Robyn Hill incorporated a non-profit organization called Virtue Inc. For Women. The mission is to provide community programming for women of low to moderate incomes for the purpose of improving self-esteem and self-efficacy. Virtue Inc. puts a lot of emphasis on mentoring and support, with programming especially for teens, single mothers, and entrepreneurs. Robyn Hill's most proud and humbling achievement was to recently expand the Virtue Inc. for Women programming to Africa by establishing a Virtue Inc. For Women – Uganda National Office via partnership with Pastor Stephen Mirembe of Strong Towers Church. They currently have programming running in 5 locations across the country of Uganda, East Africa.

It is Robyn Hill's desire to empower people with life skills that will help them improve daily functioning and quality of life.

Connect with Robyn at www.robynhillservices.com or www.virtueincforwomen.org

www.ingramcontent.com/pod-product-compliance
Lightning Source LLC
LaVergne TN
LVHW011333080426
835513LV00006B/320
* 9 7 8 0 6 9 2 4 7 3 8 5 6 *